NV 3 AE 1571

WITHDRAWN
UTSA LIBRARIES

Pears, Lake, Sun

1995 Agnes Lynch Starrett Poetry Prize

PITT POETRY SERIES

Ed Ochester, Editor

Pears, Lake, Sun

∾ Sandy Solomon

UNIVERSITY OF PITTSBURGH PRESS

Published by the University of Pittsburgh Press,
Pittsburgh, Pa. 15260
Published in the U.K. by Peterloo Publishers

Copyright © 1996, Sandy Solomon
All rights reserved

Manufactured in the United States of America
Printed on acid-free paper
10 9 8 7 6 5 4 3 2 1

Library of Congress Cataloging-in-Publication Data

Solomon, Sandy
    Pears, lake, sun / Sandy Solomon.
        p.   cm. – (Pitt poetry series)
    ISBN 0-8229-3961-4 (alk. paper). — ISBN 0-8229-5615-2 (pbk. :
alk. paper)
        I. Title. II. Series.
PS3569.065114P4   1996
811'.54—dc20   96-25238

A CIP catalog record for this book is available
from the British Library.

Library
University of Texas
at San Antonio

For my parents,
Charlotte Russ Benton and George S. Benton,
with love and gratitude

Each one of us is a dislodged citizen of a country that was never really his, but that he has learned to long for and cannot forget. The fault lines of exile and diaspora always run deep, and we are always from elsewhere, and from elsewhere before that.

André Aciman

Contents

Pears, Lake, Sun

☙ PEARS, LAKE, SUN

Pears on a sunlit ledge, flashes of lake,
how the poised world pressed itself
through the floating surface of that day,
how the manifest made its mark.

On the peeling ledge, pears leaned,
speckled, lopsided, more than yellow—
yellow squared—before an open window
through which flared a nosy, fluent breeze.

But would those pears, would the lake beyond them,
struck full of sun, would those images
have stuck so surely all these years without
the stamp of happiness to fix them there?

The proximate cause is gone. The moment stays
through the world's facts: pears, lake, sun,
become now artifacts, seeming finer
than the passing beauty of the world itself.

Even this noon I hold them up to praise
in the face of such brilliant fluidity
now that the eaves let slip their slick icicles
and snow eases again into the ground.

I

The boy, alone in a new landscape on the Sabbath,
loafs along a dirt road when he spots,
amidst mustardy pink grasses, tall
and undulating, a glint, a maverick light,
and stoops for its source among the stalks: a knife,
wood handle smooth against his palm,
grain oiled by long handling, blade
tarnished but true.
                    Though he knows, *Carry nothing
on the Sabbath,* he wants the way he'll want only
a few times in his life; hurting with want
for some improbable, immanent change, something
his, as he turns the knife in his hands and turns it;
warms it until his own heat comes back.

He knows what his father would say—*Throw it back*—
so he flings it away, watches it twirl as it falls,
like a star arcing over the stirring grasses.
And yet he cannot leave it at that: he must run
to find it.
                When next he throws the knife, he throws it
straight, blade burying in the rutted road.
Again, he'll pick it up, again hurl it,
seeking and finding the object of desire, following
what he's found until it takes him home.

Why, when the kids threw his hat on the rails,
did that boy scramble after it? The adults,
who had been craning for an overdue commuter train,
knew better, yelling, *Come back*,
Let it go, as he jumped, weeping, down
onto the Illinois Central tracks to retrieve
his hat, and for several long, uneasy minutes
he disappeared as we strained to see him. Suddenly,
all I could see was my brightly patched inner tube
spinning in the air where that mean, laughing man,
my father's friend, had thrown it. It trembled
beyond the steep face of the dune and fell
and fell into the small, calm place
beyond the waves. They had to pull me back.
I was going over the edge like this child
to save myself from loss, to save myself.
So when the boy, old wool watchcap fixed on his head,
clambered back, I was still leaning forward,
as if hands grasped my bony shoulders,
as if sobs rose in my own throat,
and a woman nearby smiled brusquely and nodded,
saying, *Kids,* now that the suspense had ended,
now that the story was known, as the boy leaned
against a post, beyond comfort and alone.

To that window he roused us, blurred with sleep,
our mouths slack with the side-on push of sheet
and mired in a dry, slightly bitter taste,
our eyes blinking into true: the full moon,
centered in that open screen and, in memory,
huge (as since I've seen it rounding from fields
or along a road like an outsized sign for food
or gas), and yet, as my father pointed, less
itself as the earth's shadow slowly slid,
like an eye doctor's black disk, between
the white, familiar O and us. A flush rose,
dulled garnet, there. Heads on hands, we waited,
toes alertly squirreling. The crickets stopped.
The warm, loamy breeze did not—it belled
the nightgowns at our skinny knees. First, sighs
as shadow hitched and held, then fidgeting unease
over the return: that it would not come, that it would.

Brown twig with a scored, russet skirt of wings,
you cling to the side of the garbage can
where the lid fits, and, except for a slight twitch
to your pointed mandible, hold wholly still.
When you finally move, it's just to shift
your strandlike, green back legs
one at a time, each leg tapping to find
the next foothold, the way a blind man tests
with his stick, seeming to feel your way
towards a next meal that is nowhere evident.
Unlike the lion as it inches through the grass,
for you the hunt is never in pursuit
but in opportunity—what comes to you
as you wait, forearms set for the next
approaching life: bluebottle, fruit,
even horseflies might do if only they'd appear,
swoop down and so, by accident, choose you,
drawn by the stench of refuse—coffee grounds,
rinds, all the sticky, fleshy things.
How can you stand the suspense?
I cannot stand the suspense, and yet
as the morning sun moves imperceptibly forward,
I sit on the piled newspapers I came to throw away,
I sit at your feet, so stilled that in time
the air breaks into hums of many registers
as it swirls and startles and catches with flies.

The man I love keeps stumbling.
His legs no longer work.
Each day, in secrecy, I think,
Today the loss will be over.
I will yell, *Time to go inside,*
and the still body of my friend
will rise, brush itself off
and the Pretend War will end.
Yet each month this man's step
grows more unsteady.
And I who am accustomed
to fixing things,
accustomed, shall we say,
to trying to fix things,
sit on my side of the bed,
looking at the fists
my hands have made.
Who would they fight?
What would I blame?

Haven't I resigned myself
to the good loss?
When I sit down
to play chess with my father
I know I will not win.
How can I hate my father?
He cannot help it,

this instinct for playing
the right piece at the right time.
I am still a child,
yelling, *Unfair, unfair, unfair*
at my father who smiles
with something like love
before he rises to say good night.

At first you walked slightly bent
as if you carried on your back a burden
for which you made slight adjustment.
Then I saw you hesitate at stairs,
each sequence of steps a puzzle
to be thought through. Then even balance
seemed uncertain—sometimes you reeled
when you stood, meaning to stand still.
So I stood within reach,
though you said nothing, and I was a poor support
being inclined towards you and none too steady.
Then to stand itself was tricky
as you'd rise in stages from the dining table,
holding first the edge of the table,
the back of the chair, then the table and the wall,
then the wall alone. Again and again
you said nothing, and I went along,
for your sake, I thought, pretending
nothing was wrong. But last night,
when you tried to climb in the car
on the passenger side, when you tried
to hike your cramped leg high enough
to lay it on the car floor and to lean
the other way so you could angle your spine
after it, when your right leg slipped
and you fell in the damp muddle of leaves
along the drainage ditch, one leg in the car,
the other buckled beneath you, when even then
I should have said nothing, only leaned over
to grab your hand and hoist you up again,
I couldn't help it—you so undermined—
your name tore out of me, blood and muscle
of my heart. Soon you were beside me

with your eyes intent on the unlit road,
willing me to gun the engine and go.
And though I turned the key,
I had to reach for your hand to steady myself
on the rock of your obstinate silence
as the other hand flicked the headlights on
and steered us out onto the crown of the road,
following by rote the pale, broken line.

We head into the full-color, half-light of fall—
one of those days when rain is on the tip
of every tongue, leaf, and tendril,
when leaves released in each shiver of drizzle
and leaves stuck in mosaic across the sidewalk
have lost their arch and skitter, soggy, subdued now,
like me, who sinks the spade deeper,
turning clumps of root and loam from a lopsided hole
as earthworms recoil in raw, distressed spurts,
their slug-laced feeding places overturned.

The azalea, which I ease from its plastic pot,
won't bloom until spring,
after the season of darkness and freezing afternoons
(so good, so necessary for tulips),
nor will the bulbs I bury, nor will the seeds
I shake from the snapdragon's brittle bells—
so many seeds they must overload the soil
already weighed down with its hidden charges:
hold the next generation to root, sprout,
break into leaf and flower; eat the dead.

I know something radical and fierce
must catch beneath this disturbed surface
even if it is only heat
as skeleton stalks, sodden leaves
settle and warm into some other life,

hardly knowable as life,
ingrained in the soil itself.

Turn them into earth, then,
with the germs of something else,
flatten the surface back,
leave the change to work.

First the call, then the drive,
barreling under a swollen moon
to the distant emergency room
where I found you stretched out
under a damp, twisted sheet,
shoes untied and dangling, pants
unbuttoned so that doctor after doctor
could probe the distended abdomen,
trying to name the cause of such pain.
I braced your head while you retched
into a blue, kidney-shaped bowl,
then hovered by your bed, babbling,
trying not to shake as I stroked
your arm and neck. And when the nurse,
without excuse, wheeled you out
into the green corridor where
for hours babies cried, gurneys
creaked and shuddered by, case
after case, we just waited together
until the fact of pain became
a high wall that would admit
no escape, no comment or complaint.

Then I read to you from my book—
Keats on melancholy—
holding your arm
as if to hold you with me,
barely hearing the words I spoke
so much did they inhabit the mouth,
so much did I distract myself
with their sound, until
Beauty that must die,
which rose to meaning suddenly

the way a tree lurches out of fog
to block the dreamer.
How I wanted to cry, then,
as you had been crying,
but when I glanced from the page
I saw you lying, breath even,
eyes closed, almost smiling.
Not an inattentive smile,
but the smile of one who reclaims
a half-remembered time when
all the gates stood wide and
much that was true was also fine.

The stately irises, opening, throw up their white petals
to extend a streaked tongue, and their leaves, too, jab
the air as if making a point, one that rises high
above the flowers and the room in which the patient lies.

The irises lean, each from its stem, bending towards
the pale orange tulips whose fluted lips spread slowly,
acceptingly in the room's heat, though the eye, impatient,
sees no motion, only, at intervals, small change.

And below the irises and among the tulips, tiny daffodils,
disordered as the sound of wind chimes, overlapping
as they tumble above the tulips' drooping leaves and the vase.
The body feels the lungs flex, the lids flick,

and the heart, hidden, plod, and always the pain—
obstruction no attitude eases. Only the flowers,
their cool beauty counterpoised, soothe and their smell,
which stirs the closed room like garbled chatter.

Asleep so early, you who once
darted ahead through the night.
I remember those conversations at 3 A.M.
with the streetlight slanting across the room
and the bright points of your eyes—
only a year ago and you seemed
almost well. But now, dinner over,
you doze until I harry you awake
and up those tiny cliffs, the stairs.
What kind of grace have you forced me to
that I can tell no one
how it is to lie here
cupping your hand between my breasts.
Even this poem rises into the room
like a trapped bird that circles and circles,
strangely calm, strangely mute,
as if hope of escape were itself contained,
until it sinks again under my palm.
O my heart, nothing will grow
from this desolation, least of all words.

II

∽ MICE

I didn't buy the old-fashioned spring traps
since sometimes the spring misses and catches
not the head but the leg, the back, or the tail,
and the mouse suffers. I didn't buy the poison
which sends them into convulsions
and keeps their bodies littered and stinking
in inaccessible corners. I bought instead
those shallow trays of glue which I knew
would leave them stuck, scared and wiggling,
but I wasn't prepared to find them that way—
the first one on its side, right legs sunk,
the other caught from behind, front legs free
and scrambling for purchase. The instructions
said to throw them out, but I couldn't think of them
squirming in the rubbish as long as it took to die.
So I poured water into an oversized glass jar,
wide-mouthed, deep, perfect for this purpose.
Then I took a tray laden with one light body,
paper thin ears and bright, bright eyes,
and held it down, until the mouse no longer moved
and its eyes stared. The next one didn't go easy;
it threatened to crawl free, it shat,
it seemed to plead for something,
but I dunked it in the clear water,
its tiny mouth working, paws reaching
around the side of the tray, I made myself watch,
angel of death, angel of death,
and the round, shining bubbles rose
from its pink mouth, moving, it seemed, forever.

∾ WIDOW

For Jess, 1985

An amputated leg, they say, tingles,
an ear long deaf still jangles the brain:
the body asserts the integrity of its parts,
and this body, at odd hours, yearns
as if his hand had passed my shoulder,
as if snores rose above the downturned book.
Now the mockingbird at the mulberry
and its mate on the fence pretend they're crows,
and their caws contend with the noise in my bones
as I stand at the window washing up:
one plate, one fork, one mended cup.

❧ PETIT MAL

All around us, the cocktail party in its elaborate rituals:
thin, nervous waiters parade in slightly frayed tuxedos
offering drinks or tiny meatballs from metallic trays
to guests who laugh as they scan the crowd,
and we stand talking about your child when suddenly,
your wine tilts wildly, your body slams into mine,
and I hug you without thinking as your husband steps forward
so that we hold you between us like bookends, pushing,
and though I don't know what is wrong, I push, push it back,
whatever forces through you, something mindless, violent, a thrilling energy
humming through you, through me too. Your husband looks right
and left and right at the crowd around us in its disturbed sea
of sequins and laughter and smoke; only then do I see
your eyes wide but dead, the snarling set to your lips,
your head hard to one side. And though my blouse is wet,
I say to him, *It's OK*, as I reach to stroke your hair
letting the fine strands fall between my open fingers,
and I say to you, *It's OK*, as I press against your tensing torso
to push it back, hold you erect so no one will know.
He tries to take your empty glass, but you won't let him,
he tries to pry the fingers back, but you fight him for it,
your fingers unyielding, like its hold on you, and though we whisper
your name again and again, it will not give you up
even to release that glass, even for us, who are we
to ask, and we stand suspended in this way, he and I,
as he looks across you at me, wanting to thank me, I guess,
so I stare instead at your face, the eyes that burrow back,
the torn mouth, the damp chin that he wipes in one gentle sweep
with the long side of his thumb, and I knead the muscles in your neck
almost crooning, *It's OK*, like another lover
in the middle of this party, in the middle of this crowd,
when suddenly you smile straight at me, a strained smile
that won't stay on; what still possesses you brushes it aside

and flows through us looking for a place to fling itself out,
not caring that it has us, it holds us here,
attentive to the mouth that sputters whatever comes to it,
it holds us in the palm of one resonating hand, in the deep muscle,
in that which sees nothing and knows nothing, humming and humming.

In the hospital lab where he makes computer models
of hearts, colleagues bring dogs to the point of death
and then, if they can, revive them, all to define
death by what it's not, to test for precincts
so close a soul could sigh across yet halt.

For the dogs this means panic at best with their chests
tamped down, and their yelps, often their last, fill
the lab where he sits, minding his own business,
or trying: the distress everywhere as close
and unavoidable as stale air or death.

Why do this? he asks. The threshold for death must vary
from creature to creature and with spirit, health,
genes, time of day, weather, season . . .
The mind—from habit to distract—hunts for reasons
but fails, the grounds gone slurry, assumptions slipped:

the subject, strapped to machines, whimpers, its heart
speeds until (an order) the inflatable vest
expands, until, the beat, pressured, becomes
uneven, then stops—until (an order) the vest
deflates, inflates, deflates, and the heart, massaged,

starts (a stalled, shaken wind-up clock)
or not, and the body, limp or not, carried off.
He wants to punch the doctor in charge, but he taps
his keyboard instead—inside his skull that yowling
as pressure builds, so many the roots to this death.

All knees at the child's table, on a child's chair,
the teacher, having traced a letter he can't read,
asks him to draw there whatever else he pleases.
Monsters of orangy green scribble out, fly—
permitted senses that thrive and gather for *A*,
scowl catcher. She praises each figure, and, prompted,
he tells her stories, inventing names, relations. . . .

A new page, new *A*. *A*, she says softly.
They look at *A* another way—a lean-to
or snowy mountain or bird's head looking up.
Bandaged finger, he says, and goes mute.

When he thinks of her, he thinks of eyes, brown,
in which his own reflection bends and moves.
He likes to see himself in there; he likes
the blank sheet and large black letters,
trellises on which his colored pencil climbs
swirling around those unseen points of hurt.
They do not easily unlearn him, so he can start.

My friend seems near tears over a man
she's just visited in another city.
Probably he didn't want to see her—
no bear hugs in the kitchen anymore,
no walks with locked arms, no casual kisses.
She says she feels *fat and ugly*, assuming
the fault is hers and that it's in her body:
something she swallowed, like responsibility;
something she must remember, like, first thing
each day, to shower, curl reluctant hair,
shade the angles of the face again, and dress
so as not to draw attention or cause offense.
I want to shake her to free her of such lessons
as she sits hunched and strangely quieted
across the booth, stirring her coffee too much.
Look at her, so tall and beautiful
when she forgets herself, her whole body
lit with a sloppy, ungovernable brightness,
enthusiasm that doesn't know its place.
Even in despair, it gives itself away,
throwing the mannered order of her face:
one eye tinted perfectly, the other smudged
because she got to talking and forgot and rubbed.

FOR EDMUND UNDER A TREE IN SUMMER

Canterbury Close

Face up, laid on the bench to be changed, little squinter,
will you one day remember what you saw: shadows
among shifting wedges of flash, that moving mosaic
doomed to dim with time to patterns of leaves and sky,
another shaded, sunny day like all the rest.
To hell with experience. What you have new, I want.
No sparrows ferrying their fears to the highest branches,
but shapes—all timed swoop and turn, poise and hop.
Nothing but light and movement and the intimate call
of sense on sense, the body open and untaught
and rapt, Edmund, bottom bare, brow puckered,
feet treading nameless currents in the air.

The afternoon he explained
how the concertina worked, his hands
slightly plump but agile at the keys
as they squeezed its delicate black lung,
I would have said he was kind.
Certainly he was shy.
Conversing with him was always work,
and though willing to try,
he clearly preferred his complicated
silences, retreating to a corner
to pull on his pipe
while his wife and mother talked.
He seemed pleased at his fortieth birthday
recently, as he sat between them
on the sagging sofa opening his gag presents—
funny mugs and books, cheap stuff.
Everyone seemed at ease, teasing him
about his mother's yapping, pampered dog
as it wheeled at his feet.
I knew his wife was unhappy,
but that was before she left him,
shaking her head, saying
he would always be a Mama's boy.
That night, I saw him as his own man,
bearded, bespectacled, amused.
I often met his eyes across the room.
His eyes were blue.
Surely when he went to his mother's place
on Sunday night, he intended just to talk.
But didn't he then hit
that eighty-year-old woman, slowed
by a stroke, and hit her again,
and place his hands around her neck

until she couldn't say another word?
If I heard that story cold,
the facts might sicken me.
Yet it was Alan who stumbled home
to spend the night alone,
Alan, adept at the bright, cheerful
penny whistle, who could sing a ballad
with abiding sweetness, its hidden sense
of loss, Alan, in what terrible pain
all night long until Monday afternoon
when they came to report his mother's
sudden death, and he made a hole
in his chest rather than answer the door.

You stood, small and mute,
on the stoop where she'd left you
with a tiny, plastic suitcase,
like a bad joke, beside you.
She might have said, *Be a good girl,*
you stood so solemnly still,
the block a stubborn witness,
the sidewalk, in all directions, blank as sky,
your face also blank, but watching intently.
And with what care had she put you there:
newly polished shoes, white tights,
and just-washed, ironed dress,
your smartly braided hair in blue barrettes.
In the half-filled suitcase I found no note;
only Johnson's Baby Oil, three diaper squares,
one pair of purple pants, two tee-shirt tops,
all the clothes you owned, perhaps.
I picked you up, a sadness I thought was hers
still on you in the smell of soap,
and took you with me to the phone.
Then we waited on the bottom steps
in the gray-walled hall,
your thin, obedient arm around my neck,
my cheek against your head,
until the policeman came.
He reached down for you,
you reached up, so easy this shift
into the great, blue sea of his arms,
and as he turned to go, your head

was bobbing at his shoulder—
how overwhelmed—
like a bottle, corked and set adrift
on the ocean, such messages inside you,
bound on the current wherever the current goes.

As I double-lock the door, check the mail,
kick off my shoes, and climb the stairs to sleep,
I sing what I always sing when tired in this way,
weary really, not with the evening's chatter
but with the pattern of my days:
the woman-near-the-willow's song
as she mourns her absent lover,
and I sing in that minor key
as I turn down the spread,
I'll weep a bowl of crystal tears.
She wants to be clean of him, hopeful again.
But I have studied loss: she'll have to scrub
and scrub until the skin breaks
before it forgets the pleasure of his touch.

A siren whines in the alley, and I go to watch
where, between my back wall and the neighbor's,
headlights glare. A hidden red light
floods the siding on and off as it turns.
Stray cats scatter, scaling walls in silhouette;
a man comes running fast as someone yells,
Stop, stop. But no one follows. I see nothing,
just the red blur that beats like a cheap neon sign,
like a harbor warning, like a heart,
and I realize I've got the song all wrong—
she wants to wash his body, not her own.
She wants to give him her grief in a dish,
once again to run her fingers over forehead,
cheekbones, lips. Let her feel nothing then.
Let her grieve so much she can give it up.
The red light pumps, the car engine drones.
Otherwise silence, otherwise no evidence
of pursuit or struggle, capture or escape.

Where lawn undulated
now, still half iced, pools
stretch long arms of flash
and shadow. Metallic slips
of sky shift there among
the softer greenish grays
and browns the sentry pines
lay down, scratchy and low,
where, by what clear miracle,
drowned grasses reach.
Heights, surface, depth
in one glance. Also, wind:
its glancing touch on water's
taut, now shivering skein,
and again, as gusts advance,
in the cast of shrugging
boughs, fingering needles.
At a loss to feel anything,
or any one thing,
with loss so close, all day
I find these crazed mirrors
where light skips and dawdles
and is taken in and down
and nothing human visits.

Across the eerie silence of the snowstorm—
no cars going by, people settled in
for the night—comes a rending sound like a shot
then a clatter that smacks of the ground
as if among these fraying clumps of flakes
a larger piece of sky had tumbled down.
The heavy snow has split the oak out front,
its right branch lodges in a parked car's roof
and splays across the windshield and the hood.
What's left lists as if a strong wind bent
and held it down. Nearby, another burst
or crack and then a crash, and again and again,
as if a hand worked steadily to thin the street,
tree after tree after tree, of its company.

A body only takes so much, of course,
before it goes to gravity. But so many
and all at once? At intervals the air
trembles as the next gives up, gives it up—
what, in limbs or heartwood, survival costs—
until street, cars, walks, and gardens groan
with twisted branches, torn trunks as if war
of some unthinkable kind had fingered trees
and trees alone. And though the mind consoles
with the prospect of new growth, tonight snow,
culprit snow, everywhere throws curves
as it mounts in immaculate drifts and depressions,
while the survivors stand, gashed and sad, in the streetlight,
and some will not survive this hurt at all.

III

The early sun skins us. He's crept from beneath
an ivy cover to stretch beside me, a twig
in straw, rock wedge, sack of breath.

The sun hazes the ground straight across,
a trained spotlight casting all nearby
in silhouette: field, poplar, ridge line.

I'm counting out days like coins, a hoard.
I'm presuming nothing but this bright effusion
outside the bicker and crush, the should and hurry.

Our airwaves play Disaster other hours.
I've raised him five. He's seen me. No one cares.
We're alive at the start. The lavender nods with bees.

Over the branch of a small cherry,
below the white flurry of blossoms,
someone has looped a maroon sash.
It seems somber, a marker maybe.
Today the cherry trees are out
throwing their white and pink confetti,
tree after tree, on the people passing,
and everyone has a half-smile,
or a camera, or two cameras.
Those not pointing at the children balanced
on overhanging branches or the man at the easel
painting a blur of trees at the water's curve
are waiting their turn to compose the same
arched branch, the same blossoms that erupt
improbably across a gnarled, black trunk.
Beyond the sash, which reaches and falls
with each gust, stands a woman,
back to the water, perilously close.
She cups a fragile stem as she smiles
at the man who waits for a moment
when no one passes. The air is inhabited—
her hair full of petals, his shoulders
spattered—and petals rise from the ground,
eddy at their ankles and fall. Hold it.
Hold it. Jefferson's dome's a brilliant
bone, the blunt-nosed paddleboats
swirling around, sky blue;
the cherry trees are not yet green.
And the sash someone might have found
snaking in the grass by the sidewalk,
the sash someone might have bent
to retrieve, waits for its absent owner,

a patient, unwavering presence
against which the rest may be measured,
against which the rest seems to move,
though the sash moves too like an arm
raised to gesture, *look, look.*

To catch light in its quicksilver glint
of hour and weather he had to cast
and recast, canvas by canvas, all day—

his lure a simple object (haystack,
say, or cathedral front) on which
the subject never came to rest,

but rather slipped, as he watched, by—
in the sun's advance, the mist's retreat,
whatever carried in the air that day.

Thus, canvas by canvas, stroke on stroke
in daily increments, he played in
light through light's impediments

so that time itself seemed caught or rather
successive hours and seasons caught,
their feel embedded in the light.

Each of these paintings stands alone,
as, in mind and senses, moments do:
the station's iron arch lofts

with acrid smoke as the train brakes;
the poplars stake the river's course,
their spindly stalks lit late and high.

But in sequence, they alert to more;
they signal movement—a passing life,
whole days, the artist's, yours,

accrued through many hours and weathers,
like a riverbank at dawn known
through all the senses as it changes.

How slight and cool the first, still promise.
How the air tenses, acquiring edge
in the full, white light of morning.

Then someone shuts the doors, shuts us in
with our air, no light but manufactured glare,
shuts us in with our high purposes,
and part of me starts to claw for open sky,
for clouds sped by wind, for interrupting
sun, its dryly sharp, incisive tongues.

The room's walls seem to run with damp
of spent conversation. Tiny thoughts
leap about like crowds of new frogs
overspilling the pond's banks in spring;
all legs, they hop wildly, colliding, going
where? I watch a man's hands open and close,
punctuating speech—in their element there.

Dampness settles in my lungs; I think,
pleurisy, pneumonia, consumption. No hope
but for fresh air. Only send me back
to the night, its high balcony of stars,
their subtle, clarifying points.

❧ DRAWING FROM THE EVIDENCE

For my father

You are telling me how
Egyptians thought the universe was made—
in eccentric orbits, you say—
and on a corner of the evening paper
you sketch a circle on which you string
smaller rings like a child's picture
of glass beads on a bracelet
to show me how Ptolemy said
the planets, moon, and sun spiraled
as they circled around earth.
How nearly accurate their theory was:
As they watched, the planets seemed to move
forward in the sky and slightly back
and forward once again.
You make me think of those who stood
night after night, whole lifetimes,
staring up, trying to explain.
Eccentrics, I think—as you might seem,
caring for their physics, however faulty.
Over thirty years you've taught me—
equations sprawled on restaurant placemats,
the salt and pepper shakers turning
with the sugar bowl to heavenly bodies.
Now you're writing out a formula
for ellipses; ink bleeds from your pen
into the crowded, newly illustrated margin
above the banner and the date,
and you know what, I don't care
what the explanation is
so long as you are telling me again—
the planets might as well loop brilliantly around us
in the mute integrity of gravity and space.

Mike, whose eyes don't work, asked us to describe
the moon glowing through long scarves of clouds;
we'd remarked on its beauty: transparent lengths
pulled across a circle of light, the light

playing across the sky in gradations of blue,
blue softening night as if the moon
were a point of touch, easing the flesh all around,
warming. *I've always wondered about blue,*

he said, wistful. He'd heard light compared
to heat, intense, from one source, or diffuse,
but color, so attached to moods, was harder
to think through. What kind of color would apply

to ocean or sky and also to feeling bad?
Blue stretched forever, I guessed, vast,
its own nothing, its own expanse. I stopped.
No power of words could give the blue we knew.

A summer night, the moon and the moon's bed,
and what escaped us. Today, too, what's so sad
isn't what we decline to know, but what
we can't, life's gifts failing to instruct.

Private planes flock on National's field,
limousines from California, Michigan, New York
obstruct the streets, furs perfume past
outside the Mayflower and down on Independence.
They've even rounded up the homeless
so the parks look neat. What's the fluster for?
Not because the official windchill factor's
fallen faster than anyone can remember.
We are all supposed to be toasting
the new man (who is also the old man),
but though last night's bands may have bleated,
and fireworks broken into red-white-blue banner mums,
spread like smiles, wide and unmistakable,
some of us still stomp into Lorenzo's Carry Out,
same as always only numb. Lorenzo's cousin
leans behind the counter, his apron brown
from cutting ribs, one stubby thumb bandaged
as he doles out medium coffee, large coffee,
black or with cream. You can sit there,
not far from the ovens and the grill,
and read about it all in the odd left paper:
what they wore, what you missed
being up here day after day in Mount Pleasant
at the other end of Sixteenth Street,
the street itself like a long telescope,
each end with its impulse to magnify
or shrink. You can sit there
and review the facts, dirty snowmelt underfoot,
and the unshaven man in the next booth
rocking himself as he mutters, almost a drone,
close to where you hunch, eyes still watering,
fingers flat around the cooling cup.

As the lens swung around Yosemite,
my cousin's face blinked briefly by
at a slant. My aunt's eye took off again,
panning the pine-treed margin of the sky
to cliffs above as if to indicate
how high, while we children, bundled on the floor,
looked queasily away or slept. I felt
I knew better (the thought rose and stuck,
like the laugh I'd suppressed). *I could press my father's*
whirring camera to my cheek to steady its shake.
I could pan more slowly than the eye
so the screen could see. What did my aunt know,

I thought, and remembered this today, idly
watching clips—amateur stuff—shot
by German soldiers as they whiled away time
behind the front—Parisian sights, trails
of refugees along the roads—and closer:
Soviet soldiers (two million captured) at Kiev.
Someone like my aunt had panned to show
how many, how many, many, many. Blurred
heads, blurred numbers—sight obscured.
Then, taken in Poland: men, the pale star
on their coats, whom soldiers run in hasty groups
from flatbed trucks to a nearby ditch. The ditch
grows shallower as the firing squad works.
The camera jerks and tilts, attempting to show
each group as they're prodded down and made to go.
I can't focus on their faces; the camera's frantic
to record the pace of execution (how fast,
how many, how thorough, how, how); it refuses
to linger or look; it will not concentrate

even on the sprawling bodies, so quickly
do the soldiers shovel them over, and the soil
must be soft and warm on which they drive the next
victims, who must barely be able to balance
before the firing starts and they too fall
to be covered with bodies and bodies. What do I know.

∾ UNANNOUNCED PREGNANCY, LATE SUMMER

She's standing, hand on belly's bulge, in the shade
waiting for her friends. When I call her, she turns,
face fuller than before, and more creased
around the eyes and mouth as she smiles back.

In this deft breeze, the leaves seem to throw
light with equal parts of shadow like the voice
in tremolo from my throat as I fight to hold
the civil, pleased line at such a surprise.

Are we not too old, having stood so long away
from the chute? She has broken loose, let another life,
let change have her. I turn to go inside,
away from the shimmer and fade of what might be,
to sit, back to the door in the quickened dark,
back to that tiny, clicking heart.

❧ ON A VISIT TO FRIENDS

American City, Colorado

I'm drawn to the window where the hummingbirds
come; the shrill sound of wings precedes them;
then they hover at the red sugar water,
feeding before they're gone. Behind, the peaks
hunch sternly white against a wide,
uninterrupted blue in a clarity
that broaches no doubt or misunderstanding
though the weather keeps coming, moving
east across the divide. The doors of the cabin
stand open. From where I sit, sounds
my friends make—wife, husband, child—
join in a blur of murmurs and thumps that become
occasionally distinct as when one voice,
one fragment, carries clear across a crowd:
this burst of hammer blows, dog bark,
that half-cry in frustration or surprise.
The whole family at work, cheered,
it seems, by their shared jobs. Underneath
the commotion, despite the known disturbances—
burdens of marriage and of child-raising—
the whole house, family, spring day,
that which is being made is freighted with stillness
as if held in a frame, fragile, carrying weight.
Before me, one hummingbird, red throated,
hangs briefly. Yet even set at the fastest stop
my camera catches motion in those wings:
a halo of echoes rounds the body as it goes.

Spit this way and the molecules flow east
towards the Atlantic, that way, towards the Pacific.

Not just another fall line, this invisible line,
but the whole continent's dividing place,

distinguished here by a close sense of sky,
like a friendly bear hug all around.

Behind me now childhood's warm seas,
those repeated questions asked of origins,

ahead, the shore of older age and, beyond,
that other horizon towards which I seem to bend.

When did I cross the fall? I saw no marker;
first gravity shifted and then I felt it.

I recall the motel's marquee read,
Welcome Future Business Leaders of America,
yet we drove in intent on a king-sized bed
and commerce touching happiness and health,

to spend our first extravagant hours
(*If it feels good,* your Cherokee grandma said,
do it to death) under a print of sunflowers,
which the management had bolted to the wall

to ward off theft by enterprising guests like you;
who decided to give me everything, all
the neatly wrapped nubs of soap, tissue
from its metal box, the matchbooks and glass

ashtrays that said Holiday Inn again
and again, stationery scraps with "Dear J" in blue,
failing ink and half an address for "Ken"
Somebody——we couldn't make out who. Hookless

hangers, a plastic-covered Bible, you name it,
naked, you found it and brought it to me then,
a funny, temporary wealth, the quiet
kind that no one wills or steals or boasts about,

but spends at leisure only: how we slept
and woke and left with nothing, I admit,
but the complimentary shoeshine cloth I've kept
these many years crumpled in a drawer

against the time when I give everything away
or when, pack rat to the last and unrepentant,
I find I've nothing further to accept
but the promised end to feeling good that day.

I was hunched to comb out pebbles and rubble—
two bucketsful to show for an hour's
scrabbling and nails edged in dirt
inclined above the palm's soiled plane
and the autumn air smelling of earth—
when I struck a black lump beneath
the riddled soil of my reclaimed garden.

I'd mined rocks that size before
and scraps of human manufacture—
pirouettes of broken glass,
bottle caps and plastic forms:
a tiny, molded train, more charm
than toy, snapped spoon, five buttons.
Not to mention pennies, dimes.

But nothing I couldn't name: round,
this, so stuck in its lip of ground
the earth seemed set to suck it in
rather than let it go: iron
and pocked like a cannon ball or moon,
but small as an orange the hands cup,
mouth moistening for the tart pulp.

I worked my fingers down its curved,
rough sides, then used the spade
to lever it free, an enormous bead
ready for stringing, a weight, perhaps?
As I knifed the earth from its packed core
I practiced its hoist and its vacant smell—
old shoes like the ones my grandfather left.

And maybe its smell or the cool climbing,
palm to hand to arm, as it leached
my body's heat (dense with cold,
it seemed, a black hole for warmth,
taking and taking so my arm ached),
maybe the pull of cold, something,
spooked me—severe, relentless, not me.

I dropped it, rose, wanting it nowhere
I was, not around where I lived, gone.
A gate thudded shut, I thought,
a weight banging on its lengthened rope—
a function, I thought: as this, so that;
as I opened the gate, so the weight rose,
as I stood beyond, so a falling closed.

I must forget what I know, I thought,
a nonthought, a staying ache in my arms.
I kicked the weight to a dried bed of mums
and perched on the porch steps, glum
for the nothing I couldn't name—wouldn't—
uncarried in my womb—that stone,
that overdue note, that newt, that not.

Chickadees and finches vie for the feeder that leans
against the window. They veer and swoop, each landing tricky,
then fly, casting off chirrups and scratches and a *thunk, thunk,*
as—their weight displaced—the feeder waddles and the pane
vibrates; their weight almost enough to make a racket.

And such a commotion of seed: millet, cracked corn, oat;
the birds beak it by in search of sunflower, and it clatters
down on the mourning doves, stolid ground patrols
on constant watch for seed—with one eye then another—
in nodding, attentive no's, like matrons disapproving

but contented. Their throaty *rue, rue* insinuates
the room where I sat for many months trying to recover,
though recover what I rarely wondered, I'd floated so far
from myself—a swimmer who's drawn out by currents and depths
while the beach recedes, and human shapes grow minuscule—

so far I no longer even looked back, but waited it out,
each swell an ordeal, like the time alone in deep sea
when, weakening, I saw two figures rise beneath me,
human sized, ghostly pale and banking like birds:
sea turtles, ancient and free. Then swimming in seemed easy.

But these birds at their lively, persistent work, I watched
all that winter, and while no moment occurred when I knew,
now you'll survive, since I didn't know I was in danger,
I busied myself in their noise and society: the cardinal
with his *chip, chip,* like flecks of light, his appetite.

Such simple work: the pen's diagonal
wedged between the third finger's ledge
and the thumb and pushed along by the pointer
as the ring finger and pinkie drag after;
their nails scrape along the paper's smooth,
white ground, but leave no trail behind.
The pen point leaks its moist, black,
meandering line, the pointer bobs,
the other fingers steady or endorse each loop
or rise. Above this enterprise, the head,
slightly bent, blinking down its nose,
surveys the progress as it orders, judges,
a well-fed foreman at work over fields
that, row by row—grow pure dross, grow
good corn—accrue, as the hand labors blindly
and in spurts—move and rest, move and rest
as thought progresses; the hand sometimes told
to strike an entire line or clumps of words,
asked to try again in the margins or above:
unwieldy words for all their fragile strands,
unintended meanings trapped within.
Before the page fills, the head shakes;
pen must be laid aside, hand must take up
page to join, palm to palm, the other
hand, transforming flat to crumpled, round.
Lines, so hard worked, bend and twist
in the page's crisp hollows, its caves.
What must be said can't be said this way.

IV

It's Antaeus whom we understand,
strange strength drawn and drawn again
from home ground, his need to touch down
through each engagement and between forays out,

not Hercules, who, sensibly, keeps
his enemy apart from what sustains him,
the hero who conquers what would oppose by holding
close, raising up, who embraces to exalt.

It's Antaeus who wins our sympathy.
Who, like us, dumbly needs what he needs:
lumpy, black humus between the toes,
the smooth, warmed slab of exposed granite;

or rather, the grayed, body-imprinted chair,
the craning light that burnishes the desk,
just the particular smell of floors or walls
that surround and protect reliably as one

who loves us well and, more, whom we love:
our own place, which we touch, which touches us;
or a discipline, an approach—mind and soul
strengthened, satisfied there; that field

where we make our stand with the sensed possible
like a big sky everywhere around
and rising through us, blood in our veins, tangible,
tremulous, an enthusiasm, an art.

Ovid takes to the beach to recite poems,
Latin rising through him mouthy and loud.
Let Tomis' barbarians turn to shrug.
Their civilized eccentric, kept from books,
works, in rhythms, words that once washed
daily past him with their subtle shifts,
their currency of villa and street—his true,
his first, his untranslatable self, dismissed.

Why must he change, now that language pools
and stagnates? Even the pen, which governs suffering,
reminds him. A brisk wind off the Euxine. Dusk.
He trails into hardscrabble fields to pick
sour fruit and picks and picks it, a crow,
beaky, peckish, mouth full of other.

༄ WINDOWS, HAWTHORNDEN CASTLE

The Norse called them *wind eyes,* and so they seem
as weather slams across the pane today,

and I peer through the ancient gap in the wall's
foot-thick defenses at courtyard and house.

The facade is stamped by windows (each different
in height and size) and patched with stone where once

windows perched, a past, a history
in changed perspectives there to be studied the way

I read your unfamiliar tones, gestures,
talk for how you make things out. What attracts

close study may just be what's sensed
between, like that wild, invisible wind, which now

my wind eye lets me see as gusts skirt
the stone and lift through sunshine flakes of snow.

❧ IN THE NEW COUNTRY:
ENGLISH ENGLISH, BODY ENGLISH

Words emerge oddly in cahoots.
Shilly-shallying when they should move,
rushing when they should pause, they turn obtuse.
Yet who could mistake them on a page? I listen

but can't hear, and the conversation lurches—
wrong note, missed catch, half my quips flubbed
from the start, quirks of meaning quite apart.
Not not my language, but distinctly theirs.

I'm too old for this stuff, for sounding dumb and shifting
in my chair, trying, when the words obstruct,
to mime response—unsubtle smiles or frowns.

Beyond the window, in the square, a man
swings and swings a stick till his dog, blind
as any, tracks the "throw." Then they let go.

What he's lost isn't the uninterrupted sun
or the jokey patois of his friends, their fingers fanned
to brace the passed jug as they bantered, full
of idiom and pun, after long meetings.

He's lost himself, the one he was at home,
the last to leave the plane, clutched to his seat
for fear his blood would freeze (the ground outside
white with flakes, they said, of frozen water).

When they led him out, shivering in his short-sleeved shirt,
a blanket pressed on his shoulders, to his plump hosts
whose mouths curved around strange syllables
of welcome, to the donated coat, to the land of ever-

after, he called himself survivor, snatched
from the tribe of the dead; but now he counts himself
not saved but strayed, estranged and numb, a beast
in the field, wheeling for direction, knowing none.

RETURN

After years of absence he rolled home,
new wife in tow, child too, his pockets
stuffed with bills—enough, in his family's eyes,
to make him rich. The language, like his old shirt,
still fit, following contours of daily meaning.
He relaxed into nuance and tense, found words
the way he knew each turn in the old town,
streets etched in mind and only the odd
glitch to remind of time intervening—
grayed heads, worn carpets in the cramped rooms
where new children giggled over games,
their history and slang no longer his.
His mother rested her hand on his arm. He wanted
never to have left and to be gone.

These never smiled, the Lenins, the Stalins,
which now present their fierce aspects
so near the ground that we half play
at covering chilly eyes and mouths.

In this kingdom of touch, a nose will shine
that once sniffed down on multitudes
in neck-denying coats below
arrayed across a windy square.

Through brief, disorderly summer, in rubble,
Soviet Man is lying on his back,
eyes like empty plates, as if
he too were studying cloud parades:

a knobby-legged horse, a tank . . .
a dog, a truck . . . becoming what?
Whatever, imagined, we cast up,
who long for change while taking secret

comfort from what stays the same.
Like fallen childhood archetypes,
familiar forms like these, now downed
and close to view, attract absurdly,

though well we recognize the forms
of tyrants—those who oppressed and claimed,
whose inconceivable loss we craved
and feared and finally attained.

Yet see how their hollows gesture still
at the blue field, its long procession
of shapes, of shaping selves! So many
of us, and turning, turning to what?

In the Serengeti four elephants rest without heads,
bodies rising like boulders from the plain,
their slight, curling trunks uprooted beside them
as buzzards fall and, greedy, rend,
and day spreads, red, automatic, rifled.

Watch for a long time the great, gray hulls
hacked at the neck, intimate loads of muscle
and blood overflowing the ground, a rose
that shocks the drab olive-brown scrub
and ground and glistens on the moving beaks.

Oh where are the long, bony foreheads,
thin wings of ears, mouths that seemed to smile
while chewing acacia leaves or grass,
debonair tusks jutting like stiff, white mustaches?
Where the bag men, where the keepers?

Ask the horizon empty of gesture.
Ask the browsing chorus that always arrives in time.

∾ FOR ERNESTO CARDENAL, WHO WRESTLES WITH A QUESTION ABOUT TURNING THE OTHER CHEEK

All the other questions have seemed easy.
You stand there behind the podium,
behind a Nicaraguan painting
in a primitive style which you have propped
against the podium—abundant green forests,
blue seas, a red sun smack in a cloudless blue
sky. You stand there without pretense,
having read us your poems about revolution,
about your country with its ordinary wealth
of turned earth and persistent stars.
Now you cross a stony question
about the death of the guilty,
much less the innocent,
and you answer and answer again.
Whenever we think you have finished
you start again, your eyes
no longer addressing the audience
but memory, its well-read pages,
its crowded streets: there the monastery
garden, there Merton's moving hands;
here, the place, the country house,
where the dictator kept his kennels,
here, the place that took his prisoners
and never gave them back.
How can anyone sit still for that?
So, as you cite Scripture,
the light of late afternoon
enters the mullioned window
and touches your black beret,
your white hair and beard.
Now something that escapes doctrine
of any kind, rises bravely in the air
like a white, almost sorrowful bird.

Your letter says you have a new job
carrying cement on the shoulder,
not so pleasant as planting trees,
but ten more yuan per month
for books, you who dreamed of ballet.

You write during the Mid-Autumn Festival.
You will sit tonight with your family,
eating a *kind of moon cake*
and watching the moon, *the roundest,*
biggest, and brightest of the year.

You write about Qu Yuan, known,
in the Warring States Period,
for his statesmanship and his poetry
of *grief and indignation,*
those steady companions against the times.

How far is the distance from my desk,
Li Qing, in its warm pool of light, to you?
Do you gather your books,
their covers stained by your hands, and
take the crowded bus to Behai Park again
to squander your one day of leisure
reading English by the indifferent lake?

Found phrase, *The New York Times*, 18 July 1993

The water is taking back its old places
though not as before—its course since tamed and straightened:
the high levees, flood control.

Rain by rain, it rises as before, only now—
restrained, rushed—it blows its banks all at once
instead of sloshing gradually over.

In town after town and across fields between
lives drench in change: the cat drowned,
piano, newly painted hall . . .

All labored investments, all pasts, gone to the only
element, it seems, and the sewer stench.
Unknowables bob there sharp and branched.

༄

Whole rivers lie buried beneath these towns,
their names applied to shopping malls or streets,
lost to memory of the thing itself,
their waters bled to culverts, drained and neat.

Yet what is lost may reassert itself
as the tree's roots arch the driveway's cool
black plane or happiness returns
unannounced to skew a numbed routine.

One night of drenching rains (the Spanish Ballroom
at Glen Echo lit for the Friday dance,
fiddle tunes leaking across the lawn)
the parking lot suddenly collapsed:

nine cars down the bluff and out the Potomac;
no one hurt. Just there where once was asphalt,
a raw gorge, an excitement of air, a sound:
the river open again to roiling skies.

∾ ∞

Two men sit beside the fire's rubble
under a night sky—its tiny, intense lights
like the notes they wring from battered guitars,
the push of melody and chords so intimate
the players want almost to look away
as, through squinty half-smiles, they note
each other's canny touch or sly rejoinder:
blues! each further riff, each variation pleasing
because related, yet separate to the ear—
made from self but freed from self-regard
since made for the other out of the other's play;
like the best of conversations, like the fire settling
into its strongest heat, as if they sat
at opposite sides of the sign for infinity,
talents quivering at the crossing place.
But what lasts? Soon they yawn, stretch,
take a last pull on the Scotch, then stroll—
flashlights catching mica in the path—
towards the cabins where their wives lie,
already sleeping, bare armed under the sheets.

Each has its center, its start,
as if someone had dropped a rock
into the black pool just there
where the light splashes up
and over us and holds briefly.
Drops of fire rise, or is it fall,
or perhaps we lean forward to greet them.
However it happens, the whole night
is moving—outbursts everywhere,
even the voices crowded around us open,
oooo and *aaaah*, the trajectory of sound
rising to full throat, full bloom,
and fading each time
until sound and light subside,
and the recovered crowd, chattering,
throws itself unsteadily toward the streets
that lead outward, outward and gone.
But the fireworks don't stop—
under the streetlamps bugs ricochet
like sparks, and leaves along the jagged treetops
dart like licks of flame straight up.
Everywhere the world throws itself away,
the world gives itself away.
Tonight, say nothing about the ends,
but reach and reach and reach. . . .

Shifting on slated metal chairs,
two young couples address their meal:
barbecued ribs, corn on the cob,
potatoes forked from blackened foil
that peels like skin from a deep burn.
Their voices rise in turn, hands gesture,
as each tells stories about growing up,
each speaking from experience, saying *I.*
Around them, air sweetens as it cools—
breeze swirls in many temperatures,
gathering scent from honeysuckle
on the fence, from loam and mildew and rubbish,
from sauce hissing on the still-hot grill.
Those voices sound happy—fine night,
nice party—but strained, oddly,
as if they can't be easily heard,
like chirping fledglings in the nest,
each a center of hunger and self
that speaks and speaks and hears little else;
when one says *I,* the other says *I,*
and the wanted answer does not come.
Now the chosen subjects change
to consumables of every kind—
gadgets and trips and current events:
what I have what I do what I know.
Soon someone will stand and motion, smiling,
and they'll go inside, as the night, enclosed
by shadowy leaves, homes, high fences,
advances silently on the breeze
and then recedes into its own mouth.

Amidst twists of shirts and briefs
lump the towels, which she drapes one
by one at the line's extremes and pins.

Already the wind slaps them up.
As the line bucks, she dodges their damp
bulk to nudge the trousers out.

She squints and works, pinning in patterns.
Full sun. The line brightens with ranged
shapes and hues that toss and loosen.

History of this life, she thinks,
her hands raised to repin a blouse
she bought ten years ago as he watched.

And there she stops, an instant, a hand
riding the line, which thrills as if linked
to a living thing, when the wind abruptly

frees a bleached pillowcase
and spins it to mottled grass beneath
the trees and spreads it there—another

patch of sunlight in shade. She stares:
A plain household scrap blown
to unexpected difference.

Surprise, delight in daily things.
Beneath her stilled palm, the line
carries its current, its fantastic load.

We two walked, with only the clothes
on our backs, across. Even today, when I catch
a whiff of pine and damp soil or wake
before dawn I sweat, cowering in the present.
What future, but the unknown blow? What past?
Caught at the wire, crammed in the snared coat:
photos, mother's penknife, father's watch.

But we scrambled through to polka down a track
between the planted fields, to giggle like fools,
to joke about new sky, new winds, new greener
grass. What could hold me, kiting ahead,
from my furthest reach? Forget the tensing hum,
tug of home, long line of language
belling in pure feeling to far ground.

My past trails me, its wake spreading, calming.
The mind chooses to preserve only what wills
to be preserved for others, I have learned.
I *can* remember those final days in Vienna

when I thought (as I walked the streets—each corner shop,
each park!—or kissed my mother), *the last time,*
though I alone knew it as my last, who filled
like a stretched, croaking throat with praise and dangerous

grief for my spoiling country. As the train crossed
the border I knew myself safe, yet imagined that place,
the first of many places, collapsed in flame,
since all then I knew was ashes, ashes.

Now, when I speak of my life, I must ask, which
life?, *when I speak of home,* which home?

Acknowledgments

The author wishes to thank the editors of the following publications in which poems in this collection previously appeared, sometimes in slightly different form: *Antioch Review* ("Drawing from the Evidence"); *Chelsea* ("Mice"); *The Gettysburg Review* ("Petit Mal," "Progressive," and "Writing"); *Harvard Magazine* ("Pears, Lake, Sun"); *The New Republic* ("For Edmund Under a Tree in Summer"); *Ploughshares* ("Revision"); *Poetry East* ("Backyard Barbecue," "Comfort," "In Deepest February," "For Ernesto Cardenal, Who Wrestles with a Question About Turning the Other Cheek," "Lost, Departed, Late," and "Silent Poem"); *Poetry Review* ("Widow"); *Seneca Review* ("In the New Country: English English, Body English" and "The Water Is Taking Back Its Old Places"); *The Southern Review* ("Tidal Basin, Washington, D.C."); *The Threepenny Review* ("Political Refugee, One Month On" and "A Rescue"); *The Times Literary Supplement* ("∞"); and *Virginia Quarterly Review* ("After Qu Yuan" and "Praying Mantis"). "∞"was short-listed for the 1988 Cheltenham Festival prize for poetry.

"Lizard and I" and "Return" originally appeared in *The New Yorker*.

The excerpt from André Aciman's short essay, "The Double Exile" (copyright 1995 by *The New York Times*) is reprinted by permission. The poem "Stephan Zweig's New World" is based on observations in his autobiography, *The World of Yesterday* (Lincoln, Neb.: University of Nebraska Press, 1964), pp. xvii–xix, xxiii, 404–05. None of the quotes is exact.

With grateful acknowledgement of the support for my work provided by the MacDowell Colony, the Virginia Center for the Creative Arts, Hawthornden Castle, Yaddo, and the Millay Colony at times when the opportunity to write made all the difference. With thanks to my family of friends for their continuing support and encouragement. Special thanks to Laurie Sheck and Peter Lake.

Sandy Solomon's poems have appeared in many publications, among them *The New Yorker, The New Republic, Poetry Review, The Threepenny Review, The Times Literary Supplement,* and *The Gettysburg Review.* Born and raised in Baltimore, she worked for a number of years in Washington, D.C., as an advocate for urban areas and for their minority and low-income residents. Since 1984 she has earned her living as a freelance writer with a special interest in community-based development and in the voluntary sector as a whole, particularly the emerging voluntary sector in Eastern Europe and Russia. After living in London for five years, she returned to the United States in 1992. She makes her home in Princeton, New Jersey.